GOD'S GIFT BABY

1 Samuel 1—2 FOR CHILDREN

Written by LaVonne Neff
Illustrated by Don Kueker

ARCH Books
Copyright © 1976 CONCORDIA PUBLISHING HOUSE, ST. LOUIS, MISSOURI
MANUFACTURED IN THE UNITED STATES OF AMERICA
ALL RIGHTS RESERVED
ISBN 0-570-06113-X

In Egypt the Israelites
Forgot their God.
They were forced to obey evil men.
So God led them out
To a promised new land,
Where they promptly forgot Him again.

God looked at His people,
And what did He see?
Drunken priests taking naps in the street,
Rich robbers in search
Of more money to steal,
Cruel husbands, of more wives to beat.

The old high priest Eli,
God's ruler on earth,
Sat and pondered and grew tired and grey,
While in front of the people
His sons broke God's Law
In every conceivable way.

"I must speak to My people,"
God said; "I must warn
Them to listen to My words again."
But all of the servants
That God had ordained,
If not wicked, were tired old men.

In the midst of the gloom
And the godless decay
Lived Elkanah, and Hannah his wife.

They loved God and each other,
But Hannah was sad—
No child came to brighten her life.

Elkanah went up
To the temple each year
To give offerings, to feast, and to pray.
And every year Hannah
Would stand in the court
Of the women, and to herself say,

"This year I'm alone,
But I do love my God,
And I come in His presence with joy.
Perhaps by next year
He will grant me my wish
And will send me my own baby boy."

Each year, like the last,
Hannah fervently prayed,
And grew older, and multiplied fears

That she'd die with no children,
A woman despised—
Until one day she let loose the tears

That she'd locked in her heart,
And she fell to the ground,
Where she wailed and sobbed out her woe.
She didn't know Eli
Was watching her pray.
She was startled to hear him say, "Go

And clean yourself up,
Woman. We have enough
To do around here without you
Drunken women, who ought
To be home with your kids!"
"Oh, sir," cried out Hannah, "I, too,

Am a lover of God,
And I'm not at all drunk.
But, Priest Eli, my soul is on fire!
One thing I ask God for,
One thing I must have,
And God has withheld my desire."

Kind Eli, now seeing
The tears on her cheeks,
The worry lines deep in her face,
Said, "May the Lord give you
Whatever you want.
May He make you rejoice in His grace."

Elkanah and Hannah
Went home, full of peace.
No longer was Hannah forlorn.
She sang lullabies
And collected small clothes
And prepared for her son to be born.

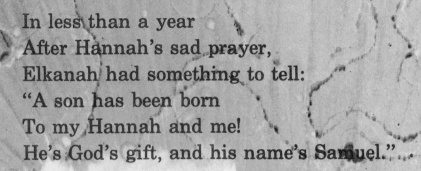

In less than a year
After Hannah's sad prayer,
Elkanah had something to tell:
"A son has been born
To my Hannah and me!
He's God's gift, and his name's Samuel."

"God's gift!" whispered Hannah.
Her heart filled with joy.
"But Samuel isn't my own.
I can't do with him
Whatever I please.
This baby is really God's loan."

Elkanah went up
To the temple that year,
And the next, and the next; but his wife
Stayed at home with her baby.
"I've just a few years
To get Samuel ready for life,"

Hannah said to her husband.
But in the fourth year,
When young Samuel had just turned three,
Hannah said, "It is time
For my gift-son to go
Serve the Giver who gave him to me."

"This is my son,"
Hannah said to Eli.
"God lent him to me for three years.
Now I give him to you,
To the temple, to God—"
Hannah struggled to keep back her tears.

"I will see you again.
I will make all your clothes.
I will visit you yearly, at least.

Just remember, my boy
(If you can, so can I),
You're not mine, you are
God's little priest!''

And God smiled at those three,
Mother, son, and old man.
"Here," he said, "is the one who will tell
All my wandering children
To come home again—
Little prophet, the boy Samuel!"

DEAR PARENTS:

The history of God's relationship with His people is one-sided. The Israelites regularly betray God; God regularly sends a spiritual savior to bring them back. Each of God's great servants—Moses and Samuel predominant among them—was a kind of forerunner of Christ, the great Savior of us all.

As this story opens, the Children of Israel are once again serving their own selfish interests. Hannah, a childless woman, also seems to be praying selfishly for her own good. But when her prayer is answered, we discover that she regards herself only as a caretaker for the Lord's child. Samuel belongs to God, and after three years Hannah gives her dearly loved child back to God. What a striking contrast to the utter selfishness around her.

Samuel was truly a gift child—a gift to Hannah, his mother; a gift from Hannah to the church; and especially God's gift to His erring children.

We, too, need to remind ourselves that our children really belong to God. We are God's caretakers and have been given a great responsibility. Just consider how Eli, the old priest, cared for God's gift children to him.

Remind your children of their real Father. (In a way you are their earthly sponsors.) Point out to them how they are God's gifts to you. Teach them to love their heavenly Father. Show them how, as in this story, God's gift of love must be shared if it is to grow.

THE EDITOR